Copyright 2020 by Norma Marquez -All rights reserved.

No part of this publication may be reproduced, distributed, or transmitted in any form or by any means, including photocopying, recording, or other electronic or mechanical methods, without the prior written permission of the publisher, except in the case of brief quotations embodied in reviews and certain other non-commercial uses permitted by copyright law.

This Book is provided with the sole purpose of providing relevant information on a specific topic for which every reasonable effort has been made to ensure that it is both accurate and reasonable. Nevertheless, by purchasing this Book you consent to the fact that the author, as well as the publisher, are in no way experts on the topics contained herein, regardless of any claims as such that may be made within. It is recommended that you always consult a professional prior to undertaking any of the advice or techniques discussed within. This is a legally binding declaration that is considered both valid and fair by both the Committee of Publishers Association and the American Bar Association and should be considered as legally binding within the United States.

CONTENTS

Introduction 4
Chicken 5
    Chicken Cordon Bleu Quesadillas 5
    Buffalo Chicken Quesadilla 6
    Grilled Chicken Quesadillas 7
    Slow Cooker Chicken Quesadillas with Pico de Gallo 8
    Chicken Fajita Quesadillas with Cilantro Pesto 9
    BBQ Chicken & Pineapple Quesadillas 10
    Chicken Bacon Ranch Quesadilla 11
    Rio Grande Chicken Quesadilla Recipe 12
    Chicken Club Quesadillas Recipe 13
    Chicken Enchilada Quesadillas 14
Beef 15
    Sloppy Joe Quesadillas 15
    Cheesy Beef Quesadillas 16
    Ultimate Easy Quesadilla Recipe 17
    Quesadilla Burger 18
    Steak Quesadillas 19
    Bacon BBQ Cheeseburger Quesadillas 20
    Beef Quesadillas with Queso Blanco Sauce 21
    Korean Beef Quesadillas 22
    Grilled Skirt Steak Quesadillas with Tomatillo Sauce 23
    Philly Cheese Steak Quesadilla 24
Seafood 25
    Old Bay Shrimp Quesadillas 25
    Cheesy Crab and Shrimp Quesadillas 26
    Firecracker Shrimp Quesadillas 27
    Sizzling Shrimp Quesadillas 28
    Cheese-and-Salmon Quesadilla 29
    Parmesan-Crusted Shrimp Quesadillas 30
Vegetables 31
    Cauliflower Quesadillas 31
    Spinach-Artichoke Quesadillas 32
    Cheesy Spinach-Artichoke Quesadillas 33
    Greek Quesadillas with Tsatziki 34
    Corn and Pepper Jack Quesadillas 35
    Goat Cheese Zucchini Quesadillas with Grilled Corn Pico de Gallo 36
    Foil Pack Cheese Quesadilla with Fresh Salsa 37
    Creamy Quesadilla Recipe 38

Pork 39
    Pulled Pork and Caramelized Onion Quesadillas 39
Cake & Cookie Quesadilla 40
    Caramel Apple Cheesecakeadilla 40
    Cookiedilla 41
    Oreo Cheesecakeadilla 42
    Raspberry-Nutella Cheesecakeadilla 43
    Pizzadilla 44

Introduction

When it comes to Mexican dishes, nothing can compare the taste of quesadillas. They are not only delicious, cheesy and saucy, they too are versatile. With our 40 best quesadilla recipes, you will be surprised at the creativity of our team to transform quesadillas into pizza, cookie, cake, or give them a touch of Korean, Greek or American twist. Most of our recipes require you to cook the quesadilla in hot pan, hot grill or bake them. The basic thing that you must do is to preheat the kitchen gadget, and prepare the quesadilla by placing the tortilla in the skillet or griddle pan and spread the cheese, filling, veggies or meat, or whatever the recipe ask you to do. Most of our ingredients consist of Monterey Jack cheese, cheddar, ground beef, bacon, spices, beans, chicken, pulled pork, shrimp, crab meat and among others. The tortilla should be golden browned and the cheese is melty, so that every bite is a pleasurable experience.
Enjoy!

Chicken
Chicken Cordon Bleu Quesadillas

These quesadillas melts in your mouth every time you take a bite because it is loaded with mozzarella and Swiss cheese plus grated Parmesan for optional garnish. You can use leftover rotisserie chicken if you run out of raw chicken breast to add a meaty texture along with deli ham.

Servings: 4

Ingredients

3 boneless skinless chicken breasts
1/2 teaspoon garlic powder
1 teaspoon dried oregano
Freshly ground black pepper
Pinch kosher salt
8 medium flour tortillas
3 tablespoons extra-virgin olive oil, divided
8 slices deli ham
1/4 cup Dijon mustard
1 cup shredded mozzarella
1 1/2 cup shredded Swiss cheese
Optional garnish:
Grated Parmesan
Freshly chopped parsley

Directions:

Combine oregano, salt, pepper and garlic powder in a small bowl and season the chicken with the mixture.
Heat in a large skillet the two tablespoons of oil on medium-high heat.
Cook the chicken in hot oil for eight minutes each side until thoroughly cooked and golden brown. Let chicken stand for ten minutes before slicing into strips.
Prepare the four tortillas and spread on its surface the mustard.
Place two ham slices on top of individual tortilla, followed by chicken slices, Swiss cheese and mozzarella cheese. Place the remaining 4 tortillas on top.
Heat one tablespoon of oil in a pan on moderate heat.
Cook quesadillas one at a time until the cheese becomes melty and both tortillas are nicely golden, cooking each side for three minutes.
Sprinkle immediately with Parmesan and fresh parsley before slicing the tortillas into wedges.
Serve!
Nutritional Information: 833 calorie; 34.4 g fat (11.4 g saturated fat); 268 mg cholesterol; 1313 mg sodium; 27.3 g carbohydrate; 4.5 g dietary fiber; 1.2 g total sugars; 103.7 g protein.

Buffalo Chicken Quesadilla

This outdoorsy quesadilla is filled with rotisserie chicken, ranch dressing, cream cheese, Gouda, Monterey Jack and buffalo dressing. This is a perfect treat for late night dinner with your sweetheart as it takes ten minutes to cook.

Servings: 2

Ingredients

2 cups shredded rotisserie chicken
1/2 cup ranch dressing, divided
4 ounces softened cream cheese
2 tablespoons sliced green onions
1/4 cup plus 2 tablespoons buffalo sauce (divided)
1/2 cup shredded Monterey Jack
1/2 cup shredded Gouda
Freshly ground pepper
Kosher salt
Vegetable oil
4 medium flour corn tortillas

Directions

Combine in a medium bowl the chicken, ¼ cup buffalo sauce, cream cheese, green onions, ¼ cup ranch dressing, stirring until incorporated.

Sprinkle with salt and pepper according to your taste.

Heat oil in a large skillet on moderate heat, making sure the bottom is fully coated. While heating the oil, spread the chicken mixture on top of tortilla and place on top the cheeses and cover with another tortilla. Do this procedure for the next quesadilla pair.

Now it's time to cook the quesadilla in hot oil for three minutes until golden brown. When it's time to flip the other side, place a large plate on top of the skillet.

Invert the skillet and slide the quesadilla onto a platter, and then slide back to the skillet. Cook the quesadilla until golden brown.

Do the second pair of quesadilla with the same steps.

When both quesadillas are done, sprinkle them with buffalo sauce and ranch dressing. Spread scallions on top.

Enjoy!

Nutritional Information: 723 calorie; 44.6 g fat (20.8 g saturated fat; 198 mg cholesterol; 2535 mg sodium; 32.3 g carbohydrate; 3.3 g dietary fiber; 6.3 g total sugars; 55.6 g protein.

Grilled Chicken Quesadillas

These chicken quesadillas are just right for someone who wants spicy, cheesy, and crunchy meal. They are packed with chili powder, red bell peppers, ground pepper, cumin, oregano, green onions and cheeses so that every bite is satisfying and worth mentioning.

Servings: 4

Ingredients

1 teaspoon vegetable oil for brushing
2 medium red bell peppers
1 small white onion
Freshly ground pepper
Pinch of Kosher salt
1/2 teaspoon chili powder
2 (8 ounces) chicken breasts
1/2 teaspoon dried oregano
1/2 teaspoon ground cumin
3 cups shredded Monterey Jack
8 medium flour tortillas
2 thinly sliced green onions
3 cups shredded cheddar
For serving:
Sour cream
Guacamole

Directions

Slice white onion and red bell peppers into rounds, set aside.
Preheat your grill pan on moderate heat and coat the grates with oil.
Combine in a small bowl the chili powder, oregano, salt, pepper, and cumin; season chicken with the mixture.
Grill the chicken five minutes each side, flipping once in a while until thoroughly cooked and browned.
Remove the chicken from the grill and let cool on a cutting board, set aside.
Toss the bell pepper and onion with one teaspoon of oil, pinch of salt and pepper; grill for eight to ten minutes, turning frequently until tender and slightly charred.
Remove from grill onto a cutting board and chop. Slice the cooled chicken into thin strips.
Oil the grates again and place the flour tortilla.
Place on top of tortilla with 1/4 each of cheddar, Monterey Jack, bell pepper, onion, green onions, and chicken.
Cover the mixture with another tortilla and cook for three minutes each side, flipping at least once until both sides are golden brown.
Do the rest of the mixture and tortilla. Slice tortilla into wedges, serve warm with guacamole and sour cream if desired.
Garnish on top with additional green onions.
Enjoy!
Nutritional Information: 503 calorie; 22 g fat (9.5 g saturated fat); 91 mg cholesterol; 770 mg sodium; 30.9 g carbohydrate; 4.6 g dietary fiber; 4.8 g total sugars; 46.1 g protein.

Slow Cooker Chicken Quesadillas with Pico de Gallo

One thing that makes these chicken quesadillas tasty is the Pico de Gallo or salsa fresca, spread on the quesadillas when serving, plus cotija and lime wedges. Pico de Gallo is a combination of red onions, lime juice, lime zest, tomatoes, cilantro, and salt.

Servings: 4

Ingredients

- 2 pounds bone-in skin-on chicken thighs
- 1 tablespoon extra-virgin olive oil
- Additional extra-virgin oil for drizzling
- Freshly ground black pepper
- Kosher salt
- 1 teaspoon chili powder
- 1 (15 ounces) can diced tomatoes
- 3 chopped cloves garlic
- 1 tablespoon cumin
- 1/2 cup diced red onion
- 2 seeded and diced plum tomatoes
- Juice and zest of 1 lime
- 1/2 cup freshly chopped cilantro
- 1/4 cup crumbled cotija
- 2 1/2 cups shredded cheddar
- 8 large flour tortillas
- Lemon wedges for garnish
- Additional crumbled cotija for garnish

Directions

Wash chicken under running water; pat dry with paper towels.

Combine chicken in a medium-sized bowl with one tablespoon oil, salt and pepper.

Place the chicken in a preheated non-stick pan over moderate high heat.

Sear both sides of chicken until browned but not thoroughly cooked.

Place seared chicken, garlic, canned tomatoes, cumin and chili powder in a bowl of your slow cooker, stir to combine well. Cook the mixture on low heat for eight hours.

While cooking the chicken, prepare the Pico de Gallo by combining in a small bowl the red onions, 1 tablespoon of lime juice, 1 teaspoon of lime zest, tomatoes, cilantro, and salt, set aside.

Combine in a separate bowl, all cheeses.

After 8 hours, place the chicken onto a rimmed sheet baking pan to slightly cool. Detach the skin and bones of the chicken; shred the meat using two forks or your clean hands.

Skim off the fat from the braising liquid and reserve 1 cup and pour into the chicken. Season the chicken with a pinch of salt and pepper.

Preheat a large pan on moderate heat, drizzle with olive oil.

Place one flour tortilla in the pan and sprinkle with the cheese mixture, and layer the chicken and sprinkle additional cheese. Cover the top with one tortilla.

Cook the tortilla for one to two minutes, flipping once, until the cheese is melty and the tortilla is slightly golden brown.

Continue preparing the rest of the tortilla, cheese mixture, chicken, additional cheese and cover with another tortilla.

When the quesadillas are done, cut them into wedges and spread with Pico de Gallo, cotija and lime wedges.

Serve!

Nutritional Information: 898 calorie; 57.3 g fat (21.8 g saturated fat); 252 mg cholesterol; 891 mg sodium; 35 g carbohydrate; 6.3 g dietary fiber; 7.1 g total sugars; 64 g protein.

Chicken Fajita Quesadillas with Cilantro Pesto

Another way to please your family's taste buds is to prepare them with these crunchy and buttery chicken fajita quesadillas. It is seasoned with taco seasoning and served with cilantro pesto consisting of pulsed basil, oil, cilantro almonds, garlic, salt, and crumbled cotija.

Servings: 4

Ingredients

1 tablespoon taco seasoning
3/4 pound boneless & skinless chicken breasts
1/2 cup plus 1 tablespoon extra-virgin olive oil, divided
1 sliced red onion
Kosher salt
2 cup fresh cilantro leaves and stems
2 sliced bell peppers
1/4 cup crumbled cotija
1 cup fresh basil leaves
1 tablespoon butter
1 clove garlic
1/4 cup almonds
8 medium flour tortillas

Directions

Cut chicken breast into chunks or strips and coat with one tablespoon of oil, salt and taco seasoning.
Cook the chicken in a skillet on moderate heat, turning frequently until thoroughly cooked; place chicken onto a plate.
In the same skillet, cook the peppers and onions for eight to ten minutes until tender; sprinkle with salt.
Meanwhile, prepare the pesto by pulsing together in a food processor the basil, ½ cup of oil and cilantro until incorporated.
Stir in almonds, garlic, salt, and crumbled cotija; blend until incorporated.
Wipe out the skillet and melt the butter. Spread the pesto on top of tortilla, place chicken, and top with peppers, onions, and pepper jack.
Cover with another tortilla and cook for three to four minutes, flipping once, until both sides are golden-crisp.
Repeat with the rest of the tortillas, pesto chicken, peppers, onions, and pepper jack.
Serve quesadillas with cilantro pesto and store extra pesto in the fridge for up to 1 week.
Serve!
Nutritional Information: 605 calorie; 41 g fat (8.9 g saturated fat); 91 mg cholesterol; 351 mg sodium; 31.2 g carbohydrate; 5.6 g dietary fiber; 4.9 g total sugars; 31.7 g protein.

BBQ Chicken & Pineapple Quesadillas

If you love sweet and spicy quesadilla, this recipe is what you need. It makes use of sweet and spicy BBQ sauce, pineapple slices and cheddar cheese, so that every bite of the chicken quesadilla tastes cheesy, juicy and meaty. You can cook it in the crock pot for four hours, or follow the procedure below.

Servings: 5

Ingredients

2 boneless & skinless chicken breasts
1/2 diced yellow onion
1 1/4 cups sweet and spicy BBQ sauce, divided
1/2 thinly sliced fresh or canned pineapple
1 cup shredded cheddar cheese
5 medium size whole wheat flour tortillas
Cilantro (optional)

Directions

Preheat the oven at 350 degree F.
Prepare a baking sheet by lining the bottom with foil and spray with nonstick spray. Place the chicken on top of foil and spread with one-half cup BBQ sauce with a spoon to evenly coat the chicken.
Garnish onions over the chicken.
Bake for twenty minutes until thoroughly cooked. Remove chicken from oven and shred using two forks.
Combine in a bowl the shredded chicken, onions, and ½ cup of BBQ sauce until well coated.
Spread the chicken mixture on the half part of the tortilla and then garnish with pineapple and top with cheese.
Place a tablespoon of BBQ sauce on the other half of the tortilla.
Close the tortilla by gathering the side with BBQ sauce to the opposite side.
Do the remaining tortillas and ingredients with the same procedure.
Spray a grill pan with non-stick spray and heat on medium heat.
Place the quesadillas, one at a time in the pan and cook for two to three minutes on one side, flip and cook the other side for one to two minutes until the whole quesadilla is browned.
Cook the remaining quesadillas in batches. Slice and garnish with cilantro if desired. Serve!
Nutritional Information: 517 calorie; 10.9 g fat (4.8 g saturated fat); 128 mg cholesterol; 1051 mg sodium; 53.1 g carbohydrate; 3.7 g dietary fiber; 29.8 g total sugars; 51.6 g protein.

Chicken Bacon Ranch Quesadilla

These quesadillas are just right for your late night dinner or tailgating. You only need 4 ingredients, excluding the cooking spray for coating to come up with a cheesy and meaty dinner treat. The Ranch dressing offers creamy, spicy and flavorful taste to this chicken quesadilla.

Servings: 3

Ingredients

1 to 2 ounces chopped chicken or Perdue chicken strips
2 slices cooked bacon
1/3 cup shredded cheddar cheese
1 to 2 teaspoons Ranch dressing
Cooking spray
1 large tortilla

Directions

Coat a medium-sized skillet with cooking spray and heat over moderate heat.
Place the tortilla on a flat work surface and spread on top with a layer of cheese.
Place the half part of the tortilla with chopped or strips of chicken, cooked bacon and mushrooms.
Drizzle on top with Ranch dressing and place in the preheated skillet.
Cook the quesadilla for one minute until the cheese is melty.
Fold tortilla in half with the cheese side over the chicken.
Cook for additional two minutes, flipping once, until golden-crisp. Remove quesadilla from heat and cut into three pieces.
Heat a medium skillet over medium heat. Spray pan with cooking spray.
Lay tortilla on a flat surface. Cover the tortilla with an even layer of cheese.
Top the half of tortilla with chicken, bacon and mushrooms. Drizzle Ranch dressing over chicken. Place tortilla in skillet.
Cook for 1 minute, until the cheese starts to melt. Fold in half - cheese side of tortilla over chicken.
Cook for 2 minutes more, flipping until each side is golden and crisp. Remove, cut into 3 pieces.
Serve!
Nutritional Information: 297 calorie; 15.2 g fat (4.7 g saturated); 27 mg cholesterol; 513 mg sodium; 21.1 g carbohydrate; 0.3 g dietary fiber; 0.4 g total sugars; 18.5 g protein.

Rio Grande Chicken Quesadilla Recipe

Fall in love with this quesadilla layered with taco seasoned shredded chicken and refried beans, cheese, green onions and cilantro. Late dinner should be a memorable experience with this cheesy and saucy quesadilla that will surely receive thumbs up from your loved ones.

Servings: 6

Ingredients

2 cups cooked shredded chicken
1 (16 ounces) can refried beans
2 to 4 teaspoons taco seasoning
3/4 cup water
1 1/2 cups (6 ounces) shredded Monterey Jack cheese
1/4 cup chopped fresh cilantro
1/4 cup chopped green onions
6 large flour tortillas
Vegetable oil

Directions

Mix together in a medium pan the water, chicken and taco seasoning and set on medium high heat; bring to a boil.

Remove cover of pan and simmer on low heat for fifteen minutes.

Add the refried beans and stir to combine well.

Remove chicken mixture from heat and evenly spread about one-third of the mixture on half part of individual tortilla.

Place on top of the chicken mixture the shredded cheese, chopped green onions, and cilantro.

Fold tortilla in half and quickly fry in hot vegetable oil in a large skillet on medium-high heat.

Cook and flip once, until slightly crisp and brown. Cut quesadilla into six quarters. Enjoy!

Nutritional Information: 359 calorie; 15 g fat (6 g saturated fat); 52 mg cholesterol; 44 g carbohydrate; 864 mg sodium; 2 g total sugars; 4 g dietary fiber; 21 g protein.

Chicken Club Quesadillas Recipe

These quickie quesadillas can be finished in 18 minutes and you only need ham, chicken breast, bacon and cheese as fillings for each flour tortilla. For the toppings, you can pick any of the choices below.

Servings: 4

Ingredients

8 slices deli-sliced ham
8 slices deli-sliced chicken breast
8 strips of cooked bacon
8 slices cheddar cheese
8 flour tortillas
Sandwich topping choices:
Mayonnaise
Tomato
Lettuce
Pickles
Banana
Peppers

Directions

Evenly spread the mayonnaise on top of the tortilla.
Layer on the half part of tortilla the chicken, ham, cheddar, cooked bacon and the toppings; fold tortilla over and press down.
Heat the skillet on moderate heat.
Coat both sides of tortilla with melted butter or olive oil and cook two pieces of quesadillas at the same time for three to four minutes per side.
Flip once and cook until golden brown.
Serve!

Nutritional Information: 702 calorie; 40.8 g fat (19.1 g saturated); 181 mg cholesterol; 2320 mg sodium; 24.3 g carbohydrate; 3.8 g dietary fiber; 0.7 g total sugars; 62 g protein.

Chicken Enchilada Quesadillas

Though this recipe requires a long procedure, it can be finished in 25 minutes. Everybody will appreciate your effort with this spicy and cheesy combination of enchilada and quesadillas, which will totally change your dinner habit once tasted.
Servings: 4

Ingredients

- 4 skinless & boneless chicken breasts
- 1 (8 ounces) package shredded Cabot pepper jack
- 1 (8 ounces) package shredded Cabot Sharp Light 50% reduced fat cheddar
- Dash ground pepper
- 2 teaspoons seasoned salt
- 2 cups tomato sauce
- 1 teaspoon chili powder
- Additional chili powder for seasoning
- 1/4 teaspoon cinnamon
- 1 teaspoon cumin
- Additional cumin for seasoning
- 1 1/2 teaspoon sriracha or hot sauce
- 1 1/2 teaspoon brown sugar
- 8 pieces 8-inch flour tortillas
- Cooking spray

Directions

Mix together in a small pot the sriracha, tomato sauce, 1 ½ teaspoon brown sugar, ¼ teaspoon cinnamon, 1 teaspoon chili powder, 1 teaspoon cumin, and 1 teaspoon chili powder; simmer for fifteen minutes.

Rub the chicken with seasoned salt, extra cumin, extra chili powder, salt, and pepper. Grill the chicken for three to four minutes each side on moderate heat until thoroughly cooked. Let cool and shred.

Combine in a bowl the shredded Cabot pepper jack and shredded Cabot Sharp Light 50% reduced fat cheddar and divide them into four equal piles for individual quesadilla.

Divide the chicken into four equal piles.

Heat a large non-stick pan on moderate high heat.

Place on a cutting board one tortilla and spread on top about three tablespoons of enchilada sauce to cover the entire bottom.

Spread one pile of cheese on top of the enchilada sauce and evenly spread the piles of chicken over the cheese.

Spread the other half pile of cheese on top of the chicken.

Coat the pan with cooking spray and place the quesadilla and put the second tortilla over the filling and flatten out with your hand.

Spray the top of tortilla with cooking spray and put a heavy thing while cooking.

Cook the quesadilla for three to four minutes, turning once and cook for three to four minutes more until brown.

Place cooked quesadilla to a cutting board. Do the rest of the three quesadillas and remaining ingredients with the same steps.

Enjoy!

Nutritional Information: 1100 calorie; 31.5 g fat (15.1 g saturated fat); 320 mg cholesterol; 3283 mg sodium; 60.8 g carbohydrate; 4.2 g dietary fiber; 8.4 g total sugars; 145.9 g protein.

Beef
Sloppy Joe Quesadillas

Substitute bun bread with tortillas and fill with ground beef mixture, cheddar and Monterey Jack to come up with a delicious Sloppy Joe Quesadillas. It melts in the mouth, and its saucy and spicy tastes will wow your guests to the max.

Servings: 4

Ingredients
1/2 chopped onion
1 tablespoon extra-virgin olive oil
1 pound ground beef
2 cloves garlic
1/3 cup brown sugar
1/2 cup ketchup
1 tablespoon chili powder
1 cup shredded Monterey Jack
2 tablespoons mustard
Freshly ground black pepper
Kosher salt
1 cup shredded cheddar
4 medium flour tortillas

Directions
Heat the olive oil in a large skillet on medium heat and sauté the onions for five minutes until tender.
Add the garlic and cook for thirty seconds until aromatic.
Add the beef and cook for six to eight minutes until pink color has vanished. Remove excess fat.
Stir in brown sugar, ketchup, chili powder, salt and pepper; simmer for five minutes until thickened.
Place mixture onto a plate and wipe out the skillet. Place the flour tortilla in the skillet over moderate high heat.
Place on top of tortilla the beef mixture, cheddar cheese and Monterey Jack; cover with the second tortilla.
Cook for two minutes each side, flip once, until both tortillas are golden brown and the cheese is melty.
Repeat the procedure for the remaining tortillas and ingredients.
Slice quesadillas into wedges. Serve warm.
Enjoy!
Nutritional Information: 482 calorie; 17.3 g fat (5.8 g saturated fat); 114 mg cholesterol; 702 mg sodium; 35.7 g carbohydrate; 3.4 g dietary fiber; 20 g total sugars; 16.6 g protein.

Cheesy Beef Quesadillas

These flavorful quesadillas are filled with cheese, and beef mixture, which is a blend of onion, garlic, black beans, taco seasoning, and tomato paste plus cilantro and avocado. It is best served with sour cream and lime wedges.

Servings: 4

Ingredients

1 pound ground beef
1 tablespoon Taco Seasoning
Freshly ground black pepper
Kosher salt
1 diced onion
2 tablespoons tomato paste
2 minced cloves garlic
2 pitted and diced avocados
1/4 cup chopped fresh cilantro
8 ounces rinsed and drained black beans
4 teaspoons canola oil, divided
4 large flour tortillas
8 ounces shredded white Cheddar
Sour cream, for serving
1 lime, cut into wedges

Directions

Brown the beef in a large cast-iron skillet on medium high heat; break up the meat with a wooden spoon and sprinkle with salt and pepper.

Add the onion and garlic to the meat and sauté for three to four minutes until softened.

Pour the tomato paste, 1 tablespoon of water, black beans and taco seasoning into the meat mixture; cook for five minutes on medium low heat.

Turn off stove and add the cilantro and avocado to the mixture.

Heat 1 teaspoon of oil in a large non-stick pan on medium heat.

Place the tortilla one at a time in the pan and sprinkle with cheese, beef-vegetable mixture and extra cheese.

Fold the tortilla over, fry both sides until lightly browned and the cheese have melted.

Repeat the same steps with the remaining tortillas, beef-vegetable mixture and extra cheese.

Cut cooked quesadillas into wedges. Serve with sour cream and lime wedges.

Serve!

Nutritional Information: 914 calorie; 54 g fat (21.2 g saturated fat); 163 mg cholesterol; 1163 mg sodium; 52.4 g carbohydrate; 11.8 g dietary fiber; 4.4 g total sugars; 58.5 g protein.

Ultimate Easy Quesadilla Recipe

The name of this quesadilla describes clearly its ultimate taste with the goodness of ground beef mixture cooked with onion, chili powder, paprika and cumin. This spicy and aromatic quesadilla are spread with cheese, beef mixture, avocado slices and cilantro; it's no wonder why it is named this way.

Servings: 4

Ingredients

1 pound ground beef
1 finely chopped onion
1 tablespoon vegetable oil
1/2 teaspoon ground paprika
1/2 teaspoon ground chili powder
8 medium flour tortillas
1/2 teaspoon ground cumin
1 sliced avocado
1 1/2 cup shredded Monterey Jack
2 tablespoons chopped cilantro

Directions

Pour vegetable oil in a large skillet and heat on medium heat.
Place the onion and sauté until soft. Sauté the ground beef with spices.
With a wooden spoon, break up the meat; stir often until the beef is thoroughly cooked. Remove from heat, remove excess fat.
Add salt and pepper to the beef mixture, stir to incorporate.
Wipe out the pan and place on medium heat. Meanwhile, prepare the quesadillas by spreading an even coating of cheese onto the four tortillas.
Evenly spread the beef mixture, avocado slices and cilantro.
Cover the tortilla with another tortilla. Repeat the same steps with the remaining tortillas, cheese, beef mixture, avocado slices and cilantro.
Cook quesadillas one at a time in the heated skillet for three minutes until golden brown.
Cover the skillet with a large plate and invert the skillet onto the plate, and then slide back the quesadilla onto the skillet with the golden side facing upward.
Continue cooking until both sides are golden brown and cut into wedges.
Enjoy!
Nutritional Information: 503 calorie; 25.2 g fat (7.5 g saturated fat; 113 mg cholesterol; 172 mg sodium; 29.2 g carbohydrate; 7.2 g dietary fiber; 1.9 g total sugars; 41.2 g protein.

Quesadilla Burger

Swap buns with tortillas to prepare this unique Quesadilla Burger for variation. Prepare the hot and spicy beef patties and cook until brown. Spread on top of tortilla the cheeses, lettuce, cooked burger, cheese, Pico de Gallo and drizzle with sour cream before cooking briefly in pan.

Servings: 4

Ingredients

1 pound ground beef
1 minced jalapeño
1 minced clove garlic
Kosher salt
1 teaspoon chili powder
5 tablespoons vegetable oil, divided
Freshly ground black pepper
8 small flour tortillas
1 1/2 cups shredded Monterey Jack
1 cup Pico de Gallo
1 1/2 cups cheddar, shredded
1 1/2 cups shredded lettuce
1/2 cup sour cream, for drizzling

Directions

Combine in a large bowl the ground beef, jalapeño, garlic, salt, pepper, and chili powder. Combine well until easy to handle and form into four thin patties.

Heat in a large pan on moderate heat the 1 tablespoon of oil. Place the patties in the pan and cook for four minutes each side for medium doneness.

When done, place cooked patties on a plate. Clean the pan and pour 1 tablespoon of oil, heat on medium heat.

Place the flour tortilla in the skillet and spread with a small handful of shredded Monterey Jack, shredded cheddar and lettuce.

Place on top with the cooked burger, cheese on top of burger, a cup of Pico de Gallo on top of cheese and drizzle on top with sour cream.

Cover with tortilla, cook for two minutes, flipping once and cook for another two minutes.

Do the rest of the tortillas and ingredients to come up with four burgers.
Serve!

Nutritional Information: 788 calorie; 42.9 g fat (14.5 g saturated fat); 134 mg cholesterol; 1168 mg sodium; 45.3 g carbohydrate; 3.7 g dietary fiber; 2.7 g total sugars; 53.4 g protein.

Steak Quesadillas

You will love the real taste of quesadilla with this recipe, especially created to suit your impeccable taste. Each slice is loaded with cheese mixture, avocado slices and steak. Serve cheesy quesadillas with Pico de Gallo and avocado salsa.

Servings: 4

Ingredients

1 1/2 pounds flank steak
Freshly ground black pepper
Kosher salt
2 cups shredded Monterey Jack
2 cups shredded cheddar
1 lime
2 avocados
2 cups of Pico de Gallo
8 pieces flour tortillas

Directions

Preheat the grill and oven at 375° degrees Fahrenheit.
Pat dry flank steak with paper towels and season with a generous amount of salt and pepper.
Combine in a small bowl the Monterey Jack and cheddar cheeses, set aside.
Cut the avocados into half, remove the pits and flesh from skin with a large spoon.
Cut one avocado into one-fourth-inch slices and squeeze out juice from lime; cover in plastic. Set aside.
Chop the rest of the avocado and mix together with Pico de Gallo, set aside.
Place steak in the preheated grill, cook for five to six minutes per side for medium doneness.
Place grilled steak on a plate; cover loosely with foil, let stand for five minutes before cutting into diagonal thin slices.
Line two rimmed sheet pans with a parchment paper and place the tortillas.
Spread one-half cup of cheese mixture, and layer with avocado slices and steak. Add another layer of ½ cup cheese and cover with tortilla.
Do the rest of the quesadillas and bake for ten minutes until the cheese has melted.
Cut into wedges; serve with Pico de Gallo and avocado salsa.
Enjoy!
Nutritional Information: 993 calories; 57.1 g fat (22.7 g saturated fat); 165 mg cholesterol; 1378 mg sodium; 46.9 g carbohydrate; 10.2 g dietary fiber; 7.5 g total sugars; 79.9 g protein.

Bacon BBQ Cheeseburger Quesadillas

This is the simplest method to prepare a cheeseburger with 7 ingredients, but it doesn't mean that it does not taste yummy. The beef is seasoned with barbecue sauce, hamburger seasoning and cooked with onion and bacon.

Servings: 5

Ingredients

1 pound 95% lean ground beef
3 strips chopped crispy cooked center cut bacon
½ cup chopped onion
4 tablespoons barbecue sauce
1 tablespoon McCormick Hamburger seasoning
10 pieces small corn tortillas
5 ounces shredded 50% reduced fat sharp cheddar cheese

Directions

Sprinkle a large skillet with nonstick cooking spray and bring on moderate heat. Cook the chopped onions for a few minutes until transparent.

Cook the ground beef, stir and break up until thoroughly cooked and broken into small tidbits.

Remove excess fat and stir in hamburger seasoning until the meat is thoroughly coated.

Stir in bacon and barbecue sauce until incorporated. Remove skillet from stove.

Prepare quesadillas by misting one side of each tortilla with nonstick cooking spray and stack them with the sprayed side facing upwards.

Place tortilla on the large griddle pan or skillet.

Spread half an ounce of the cheese on its surface and spread with half cup of the beef mixture, and sprinkle half ounce of cheese on the surface of meat.

Mist one side of the five tortillas and follow the directions for the first set of quesadillas. Heat the griddle pan on medium heat.

Cook the quesadilla for four to five minutes until the bottom becomes golden and the cheese has melted, flipping carefully and cook for three minutes more.

Cut quesadilla into wedges and serve warm.

Enjoy!

Nutritional Information: 297 calories; 20 g carbohydrate; 4 g total sugars; 11 g fat (5 g saturated fat); 31 g protein; 3 g dietary fiber.

Beef Quesadillas with Queso Blanco Sauce

White cheese sauce and beef mixture cooked with garlic, green chilies, cheese and cumin make an excellent comfort food via these beef quesadillas. Munching a slice of quesadillas will open your day with a bang as it increases your appetite with its creamylicious taste.

Servings: 4

Ingredients

4 1/2 ounces green chilies
3 cups Monterey Jack cheese
5 teaspoons cumin
1/4 cup heavy cream
Freshly ground pepper
Kosher salt
1 pound ground beef
3 minced cloves garlic
8 large flour tortillas
1 tablespoon chili powder
Extra-virgin olive oil
1 large chopped tomato
1/2 cup chopped fresh cilantro
1/2 cup sour cream

Directions

Combine in a small saucepan ½ of green chilies, 1 cup Monterey Jack cheese, heavy cream, 1 teaspoon cumin, 3 cloves garlic, 1 teaspoon salt, and ½ teaspoon pepper. Heat the mixture on very low heat for ten minutes until incorporated and the cheese has melted, stirring frequently to avoid burning.

Brown the beef in a large pan for five minutes on medium high heat, remove excess fat.

Season the beef with salt and add the remaining garlic, green chilies, cheese and cumin.

Preheat another large skillet on medium low heat and drizzle with olive oil.

Place flour tortilla in the skillet in batches and evenly spread ¼ of beef mixture; cover with another tortilla.

Cook quesadilla for one to two minutes until slightly golden brown and flip to cook the other side.

Do the rest of the tortilla and beef mixture.

Cut quesadilla into quarters and top with cheese sauce. Garnish with tomato, cilantro and sour cream. Serve warm.

Serve!

Nutritional Information: 1075 calorie; 54.9 g fat (28.2 g saturated fat); 200 mg cholesterol; 1522 mg sodium; 79.1 g carbohydrate; 12.7 g dietary fiber; 17 g total sugars; 68.9 g protein.

Korean Beef Quesadillas

Experience the taste of Korean cuisine with this beef quesadillas. The beef mixture spread on each tortilla is a blend of garlic, brown sugar, soy sauce, and red pepper flakes, ginger and sesame seeds, which adds a touch of Korean to your Mexican dish.

Servings: 4

Ingredients
1 1/2 pounds ground beef
1/3 cup soy sauce
1/4 cup brown sugar
1 tablespoon sesame seeds
3 crushed cloves of garlic
1/4 teaspoon crushed red pepper flakes
1 tablespoon grated fresh ginger
6 chopped scallions
3 cups shredded mozzarella
8 large flour tortillas

Directions
Coat a large skillet with cooking spray and place the beef; stir often until browned.
Prepare the sauce by combining in a small bowl the brown sugar, garlic, soy sauce, sesame seeds, red pepper flakes and ginger, whisking to combine well.
Pour the sauce into the browned beef, cook and stir for five minutes, set aside.
Coat the same skillet with cooking spray and heat up again.
Place one tortilla in the skillet and spread on top with ¾ cup of beef mixture, and coat the top with ¾ cup mozzarella, and cover the cheese with 2 tablespoons scallions.
Cover the top with another tortilla, pressing down using a dinner plate.
Cook until the bottom tortilla is browned, flip over to the opposite side; cook for an additional three minutes until both sides are browned.
Place cooked tortilla on a cutting board and do the rest of the 3 quesadillas following the instructions above.
Serve!
Nutritional Information: 750 calorie; 22.6 g fat (9.5 g saturated fat); 163 mg cholesterol; 2325 mg sodium; 65.2 g carbohydrate; 3.3 g dietary fiber;11.8 g total sugars; 68 g protein.

Grilled Skirt Steak Quesadillas with Tomatillo Sauce

Have a wonderful weekend getaway by preparing this comfort food in less than one hour. Your loved ones will enjoy these cheesy quesadillas by serving with sour cream, tomatillo sauce and lime wedges. The spicy sauce is a fusion of tomatillos, garlic, onion, cilantro, olive oil, pepper, salt, lime juice and jalapeños.

Servings: 4

Ingredients

- 3 seeded and halved lengthwise jalapeños
- 1/2 pound tomatillos
- 5 tablespoons extra-virgin olive oil, divided
- Freshly ground black pepper
- Kosher salt
- 1 clove garlic
- 2 teaspoons lime juice
- 1/4 cup fresh cilantro leaves
- Additional cilantro leaves for garnish
- 1 pound skirt steak
- 1/4 cup chopped white onion
- 8 pieces 8" flour tortillas
- 1 tablespoon melted butter
- For serving:
- Sour cream
- Lime wedges

Directions

Preheat your broiler to high.
Prepare tomatillos by removing and discarding the husks.
Cut tomatillos into quarters and place on sheet tray along with jalapeños with the skin side facing up.
Drizzle on top with one tablespoon olive oil, salt and pepper.
Broil for seven minutes until soft and golden. Let cool and slice the jalapeños into julienne.
Meanwhile, prepare the sauce in a blender by combining the tomatillos, lime juice, 1/3 julienned jalapeños, garlic, onion, cilantro, salt, pepper, and 2 tablespoons of olive oil until smooth.
Preheat the grill pan on high heat.
Rub steak with salt, pepper and 1 tablespoon of olive oil.
Grill for three minutes each side for medium-rare doneness and let rest to a cutting board for five minutes.
Slice cooked steak into diagonal thin slices.
Combine the butter and the remaining 1 tablespoon olive oil in a small bowl.
Preheat a large pan on medium high heat. Place on top of 1 tortilla the steak, jalapeño and ½ cup of cheese; cover with a second tortilla.
Brush the top and bottom of quesadilla with butter mixture.
Cook for two to three minutes each side until the cheese is melty and the tortillas are golden brown.
Cut into wedges. Serve with sour cream, tomatillo sauce and lime wedges. Top with cilantro leaves.
Enjoy!
Nutritional Information: 846 calorie; 42.1 g fat (13.1 g saturated fat); 76 mg cholesterol; 1349 mg sodium; 75 g carbohydrate; 4.1 g dietary fiber; 3 g total sugars; 41.3 g protein.

Philly Cheese Steak Quesadilla

Philly Cheese Steak Sandwich lovers will head over heels in love with this quesadilla version. Each tortilla shell is loaded with layers of cheddar, roast beef, pepper jack cheese, peppers & onions, and Swiss cheese before cooking until golden brown. It is totally creamylicious and buttery.

Servings: 1-2

Ingredients
⅛ sliced onion
¼ sliced pepper
3 sliced deli roast beef lunch meet
2 tablespoons butter (divided)
¼ cup grated pepper jack cheese
¼ cup grated cheddar cheese
¼ cup grated Swiss cheese
2 flour tortillas

Directions
Melt in skillet one tablespoon butter on moderate high heat.
Sauté the sliced onions and peppers until tender crisp; remove from heat. Set aside.
Melt the rest of the butter in another pan on medium heat and add the tortilla shell.
Sprinkle on top of tortilla the cheddar cheese and layer on top with roast beef.
Sprinkle on top of beef the shredded pepper jack cheese, and place on top of pepper jack cheese the peppers and onions.
Sprinkle on top of veggies with Swiss cheese layer and cover with second tortilla shell.
Cook the quesadillas until the bottom of tortilla shell turns golden brown, flipping once until the other tortilla turns golden brown.
Remove from pan and cut into quarters when slightly cooled.
Serve!

Nutritional Information: 915 calorie; 45 g fat (21.7 g saturated fat); 352 mg cholesterol; 404 mg sodium; 16.8 g carbohydrate; 2.7 g dietary fiber; 2.8 g total sugars; 105.5 g protein.

Seafood
Old Bay Shrimp Quesadillas

These divine baked quesadillas are packed with cheese-spinach mixture; Old Bay seasoned shrimp and another layer of cheese-spinach mixture. Adding extra flavor is the guacamole with the crunchy texture of chopped tomato and cilantro with cayenne pepper for a spicy flavor.

Servings: 4

Ingredients
4 large flour tortillas
2 cup chopped spinach
3 cups shredded Monterey Jack, divided
1 teaspoon Old Bay seasoning
2 tablespoons butter
1 cup guacamole
1 1/2 pounds medium shrimp
1/4 cup chopped cilantro
1 medium chopped tomato
Dash of cayenne pepper

Directions
Rinse, devein and remove tails of shrimp, set aside.
Preheat the oven at 400° Fahrenheit.
Line two rimmed sheet pans with a sheet of parchment paper. Put two tortillas on each pan.
Combine in a medium-sized bowl two cups of Monterey Jack cheese and spinach, set aside.
Melt the butter in a large pan on moderate high heat.
When the butter becomes bubbly, add the Old Bay seasoning and toss the shrimp until coated.
Cook and stir until the shrimp is no longer pinkish. Spread an even layer of cheese-spinach mixture on the half portion of each tortilla.
Evenly layer the shrimp on top of mixture and place on top with the remaining cheese mixture.
Fold the tortilla over and sprinkle on top of quesadilla with the remainder of the cheese.
Bake for ten minutes until melted.
Garnish with guacamole, chopped tomato, chopped cilantro and a dash of cayenne pepper. Serve hot.
Enjoy!
Nutritional Information: 352 calorie; 18.7 g fat (7.4 g saturated fat); 372 mg cholesterol; 900 mg sodium; 4.9 g carbohydrate; 1.8 g dietary fiber; 1.9 g total sugars; 42.5 g protein.

Cheesy Crab and Shrimp Quesadillas

Hang out with your buddies with these creamylicious quesadillas packed with crab meat, shrimp, cheeses, spices and greens. The quesadillas are enough to fill your hungry stomach with its heavenly taste with the infusion of heavy cream and white wine.

Servings: 16

Ingredients

2 ounces diced celery
2 ounces butter
¼ teaspoon thyme
2 ounces diced onion
10 ounces heavy cream
10 ounces white wine
2 tablespoon lemon juice
1 teaspoon Old Bay seasoning
1/2 pound cooked bay shrimp
1/2 pound crab meat
6 ounces bread crumbs
1/2 pound cream cheese
2 ounces Parmesan cheese shredded
1 pound & 2 ounces shredded cheddar cheese
8 pieces 12" tortillas
For serving:
1 pound Pico de Gallo
1 pound sour cream

Directions

Place the butter in a saucepan and melt on medium heat.
Sauté the onions, thyme and celery until the onions are transparent and the butter has melted.
Pour heavy cream and white wine into the mixture, bring to a boil and simmer on low heat.
Season mixture with Old Bay seasoning, stir in lemon juice and cream cheese until thoroughly mixed.
Remove saucepan from heat and add crab meat, shrimp, bread crumbs, Parmesan and cheddar cheese; stir until incorporated.
Return the saucepan to the heat and stir the mixture on low heat until the cheeses have melted. Set aside.
Meanwhile, preheat a large pan on moderate heat and lightly coat the entire bottom of pan.
Place tortilla in hot pan and top with two ounces of cheddar cheese.
When the bottom of tortilla turns brown and the cheese is melty, add the six ounces of crab dip on the half part of the tortilla, spreading wide to cover half of the tortilla; folding over the cheese about half of the tortilla onto the homemade crab dip.
Lightly press and remove from pan.
Cut quesadilla into wedges. Serve with Pico de Gallo and sour cream.
Enjoy!
Nutritional Information: 530 calorie; 34.8 g fat (21.3 g saturated fat); 140 mg cholesterol; 1151 mg sodium; 30.4 g carbohydrate; 1.1 g dietary fiber; 2.9 g total sugars; 19.9 g protein.

Firecracker Shrimp Quesadillas

These quesadillas are going to be a big hit this summer season. Their creaminess and savory tastes are a perfect treat for your team building, so no need to bring canned goods because these quesadillas have everything you look for to feed your hungry team.

Servings: 4

Ingredients

4 large flour tortillas
1 cup of shredded cheese
4 servings of SeaPack popcorn shrimp
1 Tablespoons Sriracha
1/4 cup mayo
1 tablespoon honey
1 teaspoon lemon juice

Directions

Combine together in a small bowl the mayo, honey, lemon juice and Sriracha.
Prepare the popcorn shrimp according to its package direction; place in a medium bowl and toss in two tablespoons of Sriracha sauce until coated well.
Preheat skillet on medium high heat.
Place one tortilla in skillet and top with ¼ cup of cheese, top cheese with shrimp, top shrimp with ¼ cup cheese and cover with another tortilla.
Cook quesadilla in skillet, flip when the bottom turns golden brown and cook the other side until the cheese melts and the bottom turns golden brown.
Do the rest of the tortillas and ingredients.
Cut slightly warmed quesadillas into quarters, drizzle on top the remaining Sriracha sauce.
Serve!

Nutritional Information: 453 calorie; 25 g fat (8.3 g saturated fat); 93 mg cholesterol; 797 mg sodium; 39.7 g carbohydrate; 2.5 g dietary fiber; 7.6 g total sugars; 18.6 g protein.

Sizzling Shrimp Quesadillas

Invite your friends to have dinner with you, so they can savor these crunchy and piping hot quesadillas. They will salute you for preparing this super delicious hot Mexican dish loaded with shrimp and chiles to tickle their senses.

Servings: 4

Ingredients

1 pound shelled and deveined shrimp
2 limes
1/4 teaspoon ground chipotle chile
1 large red pepper
1 tablespoon olive oil
1 ripe avocado
1 medium onion
Pepper
1/2 Serrano chile
2 medium ripe tomatoes
8 ounces shredded reduced-fat Mexican cheese blend
8 soft-taco-size flour tortillas
2 cups shredded romaine lettuce

Directions

Coat in a small bowl the shrimp with chipotle chile and squeeze out four tablespoons of juice directly from limes. Set aside.

Heat the olive oil in a 12-inch skillet on medium heat for 1 minute.

Cook the onion and red pepper for ten minutes, stir often until tender.

Add the chipotle chile coated shrimp to the vegetable and cook for 3 minutes, stir often until the shrimp turns opaque.

Place shrimp mixture into a medium-sized bowl, loosely cover with foil to stay warm.

Remove the skillet from the stove and wipe out with paper towel.

Prepare the homemade guacamole by combining in a small bowl the avocado, half of cilantro, 2 tablespoons of lime juice, and ½ teaspoon black pepper, stir to incorporate.

Mix together in a separate bowl the Serrano chile, tomatoes, remaining lime juice, and 1/8 teaspoon black pepper.

Heat the skillet on moderate low 30 seconds and place one tortilla.

Sprinkle on top with ¼ shrimp mixture, ¼ of cheese, and ¼ remaining cilantro and cover with the second tortilla; press lightly and cook for 2 minutes until lightly browned.

Flip quesadilla for one to two minutes until the cheese turns melty.

Do the rest of the four remaining quesadillas and ingredients.

Cut into wedges; serve with homemade guacamole, tomato salsa, and romaine. Enjoy!

Nutritional Information: 904 calorie; 40 g fat (14.3 g saturated fat); 187 mg cholesterol; 2148 mg sodium; 89.9 g carbohydrate; 10.6 g dietary fiber; 10.1 g total sugars; 50.2 g protein.

Cheese-and-Salmon Quesadilla

Everyone will approve this quick and simple yet irresistible quesadilla. Layer the salmon-cheese filling on each tortilla, and place on top the roasted green chilies and spread on top with cheese. Serve quesadilla with store-bought guacamole and sour cream.

Servings: 4

Ingredients

1 cup Monterey Jack cheese
2 (6 ounces) cans salmon
1/3 cup green chilies
4 flour tortilla
Guacamole
Sour cream

Directions

Pour into a medium-sized bowl the two cans of drained salmon and mix with ½ cup of shredded Monterey Jack cheese.
Stir to combine well and divide among four 8-inch flour tortillas. Make sure to spread the salmon filling on the half portion of tortilla.
Spread on top of each tortilla 1/3 cup of chopped roasted green chilies and ½ cup of cheese, folding over salmon filling.
Mist a large skillet with cooking spray.
Cook two quesadillas at a time on medium heat for two minutes each side until golden and the cheese melts.
Cut quesadillas into quarters.
Serve with ready-made guacamole and sour cream.
Enjoy!
Nutritional Information: 307 calorie; 17.3 g fat (6.9 g saturated fat) 64 mg cholesterol; 247 mg sodium; 14.2 g carbohydrate; 2.9 g dietary fiber; 1.9 g total sugars; 25.5 g protein.

Parmesan-Crusted Shrimp Quesadillas

These cheesy quesadillas are loaded with layers of Monterey Jack cheese, avocado, sun-dried tomatoes, cooked shrimp, onion-jalapeno mixture, and sprinkled with Monterey Jack and misted with olive oil and sprinkled with Parmesan before baking.
Servings: 2-3

Ingredients
1 pound peeled and deveined shrimp
Pinch of sea salt and freshly-ground black pepper
1 tablespoon cumin
1 finely diced white or yellow onion
3 tablespoons olive oil, divided
6 to 8 pieces medium tortillas
1 stemmed, seeded and finely diced jalapeno
1 cup sun-dried tomatoes
1 peeled, pitted and diced avocado
1 cup grated Parmesan cheese
3 cups shredded Monterrey Jack cheese

Directions
Preheat oven at 350 degrees F.
Combine in a small bowl the cumin, pinch of sea salt and dash of freshly ground black pepper.
Rub the shrimp with the mixture. Heat 1 tablespoon of olive oil in a large pan on medium high heat.
Cook the shrimp in hot oil for two minutes each side until pinkish color has vanished, remove from heat.
Add olive oil to the pan and sauté the onion and jalapeno pepper for five minutes until the onion is transparent and aromatic. Remove pan from heat.
Meanwhile, place three tortillas on a baking sheet and sprinkle each with ½ cup of shredded Monterey Jack cheese.
Place on top of cheese the avocado, followed in this order by sun-dried tomatoes, cooked shrimp, and onion & jalapeno mixture.
Sprinkle with additional ½ cup of shredded Monterrey Jack cheese and cover with tortilla.
Mist olive oil on top of the tortillas and evenly sprinkle with Parmesan cheese.
Bake quesadillas for ten to fifteen minutes in the center of oven rack until golden and the cheeses are melted. Remove baking sheet from oven.
Slice quesadillas with a pizza cutter into six pieces. Serve warm.
Enjoy!
Nutritional Information: 1029 calorie; 55.4 g fat (20.1 g saturated fat); 227 mg cholesterol; 83 g carbohydrate; 9 g dietary fiber; 2708 mg sodium; 6.4 g total sugars; 56.9 g protein.

Vegetables
Cauliflower Quesadillas

This recipe makes use of processed cauliflower by pulsing in a food processor, microwaved, and mixed with Monterey Jack cheese, egg, oregano, smoked paprika, salt and pepper, and then baked to come up with a flourless tortilla. Serve each slice with Pico de Gallo and sour cream if desired.

Servings: 2

Ingredients
1 large head cauliflower
1 egg
3/4 cup shredded Monterey Jack
1/2 teaspoon smoked paprika
1 teaspoon dried oregano
Kosher salt
1 cup shredded Cheddar
1 thinly sliced green onion
Freshly ground black pepper
Optional serving:
Pico de Gallo
Sour cream

Directions
Preheat oven at 425 degrees F, and line the bottom of a baking sheet with parchment.
Wash cauliflower and cut into florets.
Place florets in a food processor. Pulse until the texture is similar to rice grain. You may also grate the cauliflower if you wish.
Place processed florets in a heat proof bowl, microwave on high for six minutes, squeeze out excess liquid using paper towels.
Combine in a medium-sized bowl the eggs, processed cauliflower, oregano, paprika and Monterey Jack cheese and sprinkle with salt and pepper.
Prepare the tortillas by forming the cauliflower mixture into circles right on the baking sheet.
Bake for fifteen to twenty minutes until golden brown.
Spread on half top part of individual cauliflower tortilla with cheddar cheese and green onions. Fold the empty side of tortilla over the cheese.
Do this step with the remaining tortilla, cheddar and green onions.
Bake for five minutes until the cheese has melted. Drizzle with Pico de Gallo and sour cream if you wish.
Serve!
Nutritional Information: 406 calorie; 20.2 g fat (10.7 g saturated fat); 139 mg cholesterol; 852 mg sodium; 26.4 g carbohydrate; 11.2 g dietary fiber; 10.8 g total sugars; 35.7 g protein.

Spinach-Artichoke Quesadillas

Vegetarians will appreciate these crunchy and flavorful quesadillas filled with cream cheese, spinach-artichoke mixture, Monterey Jack, and red pepper flakes. You don't need to rush home as you can prepare this dish in ten minutes only.

Servings: 4

Ingredients

2 garlic cloves
1/2 chopped onion
15 ounces drained and chopped artichoke hearts
3 tablespoons olive oil
1 cup shredded Monterey Jack
5 cups baby spinach
Pinch of red pepper flakes
4 ounces softened cream cheese
4 flour tortillas

Directions

Heat two tablespoons vegetable oil in a large pan on moderate heat and sauté the onions until translucent.

Stir-fry the garlic for thirty seconds until aromatic. Stir in spinach, tossing to coat well for 1 to 2 minutes until wilted.

Stir artichoke hearts for a few seconds. Remove pan immediately from heat.

Wipe pan with paper towel and heat the remaining olive oil on moderate heat. While heating the pan, assemble the quesadillas by spreading two tablespoons cream cheese on each top.

Place half of spinach-artichoke mixture on top of cream cheese, top with ½ cup of shredded cheese, top with small pinch red pepper flakes, and place another tortilla on top of flakes.

Repeat the procedure to build another quesadillas.

Slowly transfer quesadilla to the pan and cook one at a time for three minutes, until golden brown.

Flip to cook the other side for two minutes until golden-brown.

Serve!

Nutritional Information: 335 calorie; 23.7 g fat (9.2 g saturated fat); 39 mg cholesterol; 270 mg sodium; 26.1 g carbohydrate; 8.4 g dietary fiber; 2.1 g total sugars; 10.1 g protein.

Cheesy Spinach-Artichoke Quesadillas

Level up your spinach-artichoke quesadilla recipe by infusing red wine into your spinach filling, which consist of shallot, spinach, artichoke hearts, red pepper flakes, sun-dried tomatoes, parsley, pepper and olive oil. Spread the mixture on the tortilla and top with cheese.

Servings: 4

Ingredients
1 minced clove garlic
4 tablespoons extra-virgin olive oil, divided
1 (5 ounces) bag baby spinach
1 large minced shallot, divided
1/2 teaspoon crushed red pepper flakes
1 (14 ounces) can drained and chopped artichoke hearts
Freshly ground black pepper
Kosher salt
2 teaspoons red wine vinegar
2 tablespoons freshly chopped parsley
1/2 cup oil-packed drained and chopped sun-dried tomatoes
2 cups shredded Monterey Jack, divided
8 flour tortillas

Directions
Heat 1 tablespoon of olive oil in a large frying pan over moderate high heat and sauté the garlic and half of the shallot. Cook for 1 minute until fragrant.
Sauté the spinach for three minutes until wilted followed by artichoke hearts and crushed red pepper flakes. Cook for two minutes and sprinkle with salt and pepper. Remove the extra liquid by placing the mixture in a strainer and push down using a wooden spoon or paper towels. Set aside.
Combine in a small bowl the remaining half shallot, sun-dried tomatoes, red wine vinegar, 1 ½ tablespoons of olive oil, parsley, salt and pepper.
Fold the mixture into the spinach-artichoke filling.
Place tortillas on a large cutting board and spread one-fourth of the spinach-artichoke filling on four tortilla pieces. Top with half cup of cheese and cover with another tortilla.
Mist the topmost tortilla with the remaining 1 ½ tablespoons olive oil.
Cook quesadillas one at a time in a large pan on medium high heat for two to three minutes each side until golden-brown and the cheese has melted. Cut into quarters. Serve!
Nutritional Information: 439 calorie; 21.4 g fat (4.7 g saturated fat); 12 mg cholesterol; 1585 mg sodium; 48.2 g carbohydrate; 18.7 g dietary fiber; 4 g total sugars; 14.4 g protein.

Greek Quesadillas with Tsatziki

What happens when Mexican and Greek cuisines are combined together? The answer is a great combination with the introduction of tangy and savory Tsatziki sauce, which is a mixture of garlic, Greek yoghurt, dill, cucumber, pepper, lemon juice and olive oil.

Servings: 2

Ingredients

For the quesadillas:
2 finely chopped scallions or spring onions
7 ounces fresh spinach
2.5 ounces feta cheese
1 tablespoon chopped fresh dill
Salt and pepper for seasoning
4 flour tortillas
3 sun-dried tomatoes chopped (optional)
Olive oil

For the Tsatziki sauce:
1 finely chopped cloves garlic
1 cup Greek yoghurt
1 teaspoon chopped dill
1 medium finely diced cucumber
Black pepper
2 squeezes lemon juice
Drizzle of olive oil

Directions

Wilt the washed spinach down in microwave for several minutes.
Squeeze out excess water by pressing hard into a colander and shake.
Place wilted spinach in a large mixing bowl. Add to the bowl the scallions or spring onions, sun-dried tomatoes (optional), fresh dill and crumble in the feta cheese to mix together.
Prepare the Tsatziki by combining in a small bowl the yogurt, cucumber, fresh dill, lemon juice and garlic.
Sprinkle on top with freshly ground black pepper and mist with olive oil. Heat up a large frying pan.
Place half of spinach mixture on top of two tortillas and place on top with another two tortillas.
Press lightly and put one of the rounds in the frying pan; drizzle with olive oil.
Cook until crisp browned, flip once and cook the other side for 1 to 2 minutes.
Do the second round with the same steps. Slice individual rounds into six wedges.
Serve with Tsatziki sauce.
Enjoy!

Nutritional Information: 413 calorie; 14 g fat (7 g saturated fat); 38 mg cholesterol; 944 mg sodium; 46 g carbohydrate; 5 g dietary fiber; 12 g total sugars; 25 g protein.

Corn and Pepper Jack Quesadillas

These cheesy quesadillas are a healthy option while having fun outdoors. Grill the corn first and prepare the tortilla by spreading the Monterey Jack cheese, hot salsa, minced green onions and corn kernels on each tortilla and grill. Serve slices of quesadilla with romaine salad.

Servings: 4

Ingredients
4 low-fat burrito-size flour tortillas
3 large ears corn
1/2 cup mild or medium-hot salsa
4 ounces reduced-fat Monterey Jack cheese
1 tablespoon cider vinegar
1 head romaine lettuce
2 green onions
1 tablespoon olive oil
1/4 teaspoon salt
1/2 teaspoon coarsely ground pepper

Directions
Preheat outdoor gas grill or build a charcoal fire for direct grilling on moderate high heat.
Place corn on top of hot grill rack and cover the grill. Cook for ten to fifteen minutes until brown spots start to form, turning often to prevent burning.
Place grilled corn on a plate and let cool. Cut corn kernel from cobs using a sharp knife.
Lay tortillas on a clean surface. Equally divide the Monterey Jack cheese, hot salsa, minced green onions and corn kernels on the half part of each tortilla pieces.
Fold over filling to create four quesadillas. Grill quesadillas for one to two minutes, turning often, until both sides are browned.
Place warm quesadillas on top of cutting board and cut into three pieces.
Prepare romaine salad by tossing romaine lettuce with vinegar, oil, salt and pepper.
Serve hot quesadillas with salad.
Enjoy!
Nutritional Information: 377 calorie; 14.2 g fat (6.1 g saturated fat); 25 mg cholesterol; 976 mg sodium; 60.5 g carbohydrate; 15.1 g dietary fiber; 7.8 g total sugars; 17.5 g protein.

Goat Cheese Zucchini Quesadillas with Grilled Corn Pico de Gallo

Quesadillas served with grilled corn Pico de Gallo would be a fun way to satisfy a hungry crowd. Each tortilla is layered with Monterey Jack cheese, grilled squash and zucchini slices, crumble goat cheese and cooked in olive oil. The corn is grilled first before mixing with the Pico de Gallo ingredients.

Servings: 4

Ingredients
2 ears corn (remove husks)
Kosher salt
5 tablespoons extra-virgin olive oil, divided
1 small thinly sliced squash
1 small thinly sliced zucchini
Freshly ground black pepper
1/4 small finely chopped red onion
1/2 pint quartered grape tomatoes
1/2 small minced jalapeño (optional)
1/4 cup finely chopped fresh cilantro
8 (8-inch) whole-wheat flour tortillas
Juice of 1/2 lime
4 ounces crumbled goat cheese
8 ounces shredded Monterey Jack cheese

Directions
Preheat grill pan on high heat. Remove husk of corn and rub with one tablespoon of olive oil; season with salt and pepper.
Place on hot grill and cook for nine minutes, turning the sides every three minutes until soft and lightly charred sides. Let cool on a plate.
Toss squash and zucchini in a medium bowl with two tablespoons of olive oil, salt and pepper.
Neatly arrange the vegetables on grill pan in a single layer and grill for two minutes each side until grill marks are visible and the flesh is soft.
Place grilled veggies in a bowl and grill all slices and slightly cool.
Remove corn kernels from cobs and place in a large mixing bowl. Add to the bowl the tomatoes, cilantro, red onion, lime juice, 1 tablespoon of oil and jalapeño (optional), salt and pepper.
Place flour tortillas on a work surface and spread an equal amount of Monterrey Jack cheese on each tortilla.
Place on top the grilled squash and zucchini slices in single layer on top of cheese on each tortilla, and then crumble goat cheese over the vegetable slices on each tortilla. Cover with another tortilla; lightly pressing down.
Place a large non-stick pan on the stove over medium high heat and coat with 1 tablespoon of olive oil.
Place each quesadilla on the greased pan, cook for two minutes each side, flipping once, until browned and the cheeses have melted.
Repeat with the remaining quesadillas and slice into wedges.
Serve each slice with corn Pico de Gallo.
Enjoy!
Nutritional Information: 858 calorie; 50.9 g fat (21.5 g saturated fat); 80 mg cholesterol;1219 mg sodium; 72.7 g carbohydrate; 12.1 g total sugars; 34.3 g protein.

Foil Pack Cheese Quesadilla with Fresh Salsa

This is the simplest way to prepare quesadilla outdoors. Place tortilla on top of foil and spread the Tex-Mex cheese and seal before grilling for five minutes. When done, serve foil pack cheese quesadilla with your homemade salsa, which is a combination of tomato, juice of ½ lime, cilantro, and onion.

Servings: 1

Ingredients

1/4 chopped red onion
1 diced tomato
1/2 lime
Small handful chopped cilantro
1/2 cup shredded Tex-Mex cheese
1 large tortilla

Directions

Combine in a medium-sized bowl the tomato, juice of ½ lime, cilantro, and onion, set aside.
Divide foil into two pieces about 12"by18" and put on top of another.
Place the tortilla on top of foil, and spread half of tortilla with Tex-Mex cheese.
Fold tortilla, folding up packet to seal tightly.
Place packet on hot grill and cook for five minutes, flip at least once. Remove the packet from grill, let cool slightly.
Unfold and top with tomato salsa.
Serve!

Nutritional Information: 230 calorie; 7.7 g fat (3.5 g saturated fat); 13 mg cholesterol; 526 mg sodium; 34 g carbohydrate; 3.5 g dietary fiber; 4.6 g total sugars; 8.8 g protein.

Creamy Quesadilla Recipe

Have an enjoyable weeknight dinner with this creamylicious quesadilla. The perfect creaminess is due to the great combination of sour cream seasoning mix, sour cream, Monterey Jack cheese, cheddar cheese with green chilies and cilantro for spicy appeal.

Servings: 4

Ingredients

1 (1 ounce) package sour cream seasoning mix
1 cup sour cream
1/4 cup chopped cilantro
1 (4.5 ounces) can chopped green chilies
1 cup shredded Monterey Jack cheese
1 cup shredded cheddar cheese
10 pieces 6" tortillas

Directions

Combine in a medium-sized bowl the seasoning mix and sour cream, reserving ¼ cup for later use.

Add the cilantro and green chiles to the sour cream mixture; mix until incorporated.

Stir in cheddar and Monterey Jack cheeses. Spread on top of tortilla about 1/3 cup of the cheese-sour cream mixture.

Place on top with another tortilla. Spray preheated griddle with nonstick cooking spray.

Place quesadillas on the hot griddle over medium low heat.

Cook and flip until both sides are nicely browned.

Repeat with the remaining five tortillas by following the same procedure. Let quesadillas stand for five minutes.

Cut into wedges and garnish with the reserved ¼ cup of sour cream mixture. Serve!

Nutritional Information: 560 calorie; 35.7 g fat (20.1 g saturated fat); 80 mg cholesterol; 1569 mg sodium; 34.4 g carbohydrate; 1.1 g dietary fiber; 1.7 g total sugars; 19.6 g protein.

Pork
Pulled Pork and Caramelized Onion Quesadillas

Caramelized onions and pulled pork make these quesadillas an all-time favorite. The hidden secret why they taste so good is to cook the onion in butter and olive oil until caramelized, and then seasoned with sugar, salt and pepper. Never forget to serve quesadillas with BBQ sauce.

Servings: 4

Ingredients
1 teaspoon olive oil
3 tablespoons butter, divided
Pinch of brown sugar
1 large sliced yellow onion
8 small tortillas
Pinch of salt and pepper
2 cups shredded Monterey jack cheese
2 cups cooked pulled pork
For dipping:
Barbecue sauce

Directions
Melt in a large skillet 1 tablespoon of butter on medium low heat.
Pour the olive oil and cook the onions for thirty minutes until caramelized and golden brown.
Sprinkle with a pinch of brown sugar, salt and pepper. Remove skillet from heat, set aside.
Place 4 tortillas on a clean work surface and spread each with equal amount of cheese.
Evenly spread caramelized onions on top of cheese and pulled pork on top of onions; cover with a second tortilla.
Heat ½ tablespoon of butter in a large pan on medium heat until melted.
Cook quesadilla in batches for two to four minutes until the bottom turns golden-brown.
Flip and cook the opposite side for two to four minutes until the cheese has melted.
Do the rest of quesadillas and slice into four quarters. Drizzle with BBQ sauce. Serve!

Nutritional Information: 1913 calorie; 85 g fat (46.4 g saturated fat); 393 mg cholesterol; 3726 mg sodium; 100 g carbohydrate; 2.8 g dietary fiber; 52 g total sugars; 94.4 g protein.

Cake & Cookie Quesadilla
Caramel Apple Cheesecakeadilla

This quesadilla can be finished in fifteen minutes as you only need to brush the tortilla with butter and the other side with cream mixture before placing on top the apples and cook in hot skillet. Drizzle with homemade caramel sauce.

Servings: 1

Ingredients

1 thinly sliced Granny Smith apple
2 teaspoons sugar
1/3 cup softened cream cheese
2 pieces 8" flour tortillas
Butter for greasing
Caramel sauce for drizzling

Directions

Preheat a large nonstick pan on moderate heat.
Mix together in a small bowl the cream cheese and 1 teaspoon sugar. Set aside.
Brush exterior of tortillas with pat of butter. Slather the inside of another tortilla with cream cheese mixture.
Place tortilla in a skillet with cream cheese side facing up and arrange on top the sliced apples. Place the other tortilla with butter side facing up.
Cook for three minutes until crisp golden, flip once and cook for two minutes longer until golden and the cream cheese mixture is thoroughly warmed.
Remove tortilla from heat and sprinkle on top with 1 teaspoon sugar.
Drizzle with caramel sauce. Cut into wedges and serve.
Enjoy!
Nutritional Information: 955 calorie; 40.5 g fat (23.6 g saturated fat); 96 mg cholesterol; 1603 mg sodium; 135.9 g carbohydrate; 7.8 g dietary fiber; 33.4 g total sugars; 17.1 g protein.

Cookiedilla

Go crazy with this Cookiedilla that looks like a real quesadilla and done in 25 minutes. This recipe uses cookie dough in place of tortillas and the bottom is coated with marshmallow crème and the second dough is coated with chocolate fudge sauce and placed on top of each other and baked.

Servings: 4 slices

Ingredients

1/2 cup chocolate fudge sauce
1/2 cup marshmallow crème
1/2 (16.5 ounces) package refrigerated chocolate chip cookie dough

Directions

Preheat oven at 350° Fahrenheit.
Prepare your baking sheet by lining the bottom with parchment paper.
Divide chocolate chip cookie dough into equal size balls. Place balls on prepared baking sheet and flatten out separately into big disks to resemble flour tortilla.
Bake disks for fifteen to twenty minutes until thoroughly cooked and golden brown.
Let stand on baking sheet for ten minutes and cool on wire rack while the oven is on.
Spread on the bottom of cookie with marshmallow crème while spreading the chocolate fudge sauce on the bottom of the second cookie.
Place second cookie on top of marshmallow crème with chocolate side facing down.
Bake for three to four minutes until warmed thoroughly.
Slice into four and serve.
Enjoy!
Nutritional Information: 752 calorie; 36.1 g fat (14.4 g saturated fat); 72 mg cholesterol; 496 mg sodium; 110.4 g carbohydrate; 5.2 g dietary fiber; 69 g total sugars; 5.4 g protein.

Oreo Cheesecakeadilla

Surprise your loved ones with these gooey Cheesecakeadilla, which makes use of Oreos and cream cheese as filling. The outside of one tortilla is dabbed with butter and place on top of the other tortilla with the Oreo filling facing up. Crushed Oreos are spread on top of the buttered side when serving.

Servings: 4 slices

Ingredients

1/4 cup crushed Oreos
Additional Oreos for garnish
1/3 cup softened cream cheese
Pat of butter
1 teaspoon sugar
2 pieces 8-inch flour tortillas

Directions

Place on medium heat a large nonstick pan.
Mix together in a small bowl the crushed Oreos and cream cheese.
Coat the exterior part of tortillas with a pat of butter while slathering the interior with Oreo-cream cheese mixture.
Place Cheesecakeadilla in the skillet with cheese side facing up and cover with the other tortilla with butter side facing up.
Cook for three minutes until golden-crisp, flipping once and cook the opposite side for two minutes.
Remove Cheesecakeadilla from heat and sprinkle with sugar.
Sprinkle with crushed Oreos.
Enjoy!
Nutritional Information: 113 calorie; 8.2 g fat (5 g saturated fat); 24 mg cholesterol; 78 mg sodium; 8.2 g carbohydrate; 0.9 g dietary fiber; 1.9 g total sugars; 2.2 g protein.

Raspberry-Nutella Cheesecakeadilla

These faux quesadilla is filled with Nutella-cream cheese mixture and the raspberry sauce is spooned over to bathe the Cheesecakeadilla to your sweet tooth's delight. Instead of the usual meat and vegetable filling, this recipe reshapes your thoughts about quesadilla.

Servings: 4 slices

Ingredients

2 tablespoons Nutella
1 cup raspberries
1/3 cup softened cream cheese
2 teaspoons sugar
2 pieces 8-inch flour tortillas
Pat of butter for greasing

Directions

Combine in a saucepan the raspberries with 1 teaspoon of sugar; cook and stir on low heat for five minutes until the berries are broken down and thickened.
Remove saucepan from heat, let raspberries cool. Set aside.
Combine in a small bowl the Nutella and cream cheese, set aside.
Heat a large nonstick pan on moderate heat.
Coat the outsides of tortillas with a pat of butter; slathering the inside with Nutella-cream cheese mixture.
Place tortilla in the pan with cream cheese side up and top with the other tortilla with the butter side up.
Cook Cheesecakeadilla for three minutes until golden-crisp. Flip the other side and cook for two minutes until golden-crisp.
Remove Cheesecakeadilla from heat and sprinkle with the last batch of sugar.
Spoon the raspberry spoon to coat the Cheesecakeadilla all over.
Cut into wedges and serve.
Enjoy!
Nutritional Information: 127 calorie; 8.4 g fat (5 g saturated fat); 24 mg cholesterol; 63 mg sodium; 11.7 g carbohydrate; 2.8 g dietary fiber; 3.7 g total sugars; 2.5 g protein.

Pizzadilla

When preparing quesadilla, do not limit yourself with the regular recipes; instead recreate your own recipe by getting the idea from this Pizzadilla. Yup, the taste is Italian, but the appearance resembles of a real quesadilla.

Servings: 4 slices

Ingredients

2 medium flour tortillas
1 tablespoon extra-virgin olive oil
2 minced cloves garlic
1/3 cup pizza sauce
1/2 cup freshly grated Parmesan
1 cup shredded mozzarella
1/4 teaspoon Italian seasoning
1/3 cup sliced pepperoni

For garnish:
Freshly chopped parsley

Directions

Preheat broiler and heat oil in a large heat-proof skillet on medium heat.

Place one tortilla to the skillet, spread half of pizza sauce.

Spread garlic on top of pizza sauce and sprinkle on top of garlic with half of mozzarella cheese, Parmesan cheese, pepperoni and Italian seasoning. Cover with another tortilla.

Cook Pizzadilla until golden-crisp and the cheese melts. Flip Pizzadilla by covering the skillet with a large plate; invert the skillet to transfer Pizzadilla onto a large plate. Slide the Pizzadilla back to the skillet with the cooked-side facing up.

Sprinkle on top with the last batch of pizza sauce, mozzarella cheese, Parmesan cheese, pepperoni, and Italian seasoning.

Put the skillet on top of the broiler and cook for two minutes until the pepperoni is crisp-tender and the cheese melt.

Sprinkle parsley on top.

Serve!

Nutritional Information: 242 calorie; 16.8 g fat (6.4 g saturated fat); 36 mg cholesterol; 744 mg sodium; 8.6 g carbohydrate; 1.2 g dietary fiber; 0.9 g total sugars; 14.4 g protein.

www.ingramcontent.com/pod-product-compliance
Lightning Source LLC
Chambersburg PA
CBHW081129080526
44587CB00021B/3805